Making and dyeing acrylic jewellery
Sarah Packington

Published by Morse-Brown Publishing
Series Editor: John Morse-Brown
Photography © Morse-Brown Design Limited
Design & Production: Morse-Brown Design Limited.
↗ www.morsebrowndesign.co.uk
For more titles in this series, see ↗ www.how2crafts.com

ISBN: 978-0-9550241-8-4

Printed in the UK by John Price Printers

This is more than just a book...

This is the start of a conversation about making and dyeing acrylic jewellery.
By buying this book, you've joined that conversation, and we'd love to hear from you...

In this book you'll find photographic step-by-step instructions that will enable you to make and dye your own acrylic jewellery. But unlike most books you buy, it doesn't stop there. Once you've had a go at making acrylic jewellery yourself, you can upload and share photos of your creations, and any comments and ideas, onto our website at ↗ **www.how2crafts.com**. Then, once we've come to the end of our print run for this book, we'll select the best photos and comments and include them in the new edition of the book as a 'reader's appendix' – a source of inspiration and alternative designs for future readers.

As we've said on the how2crafts website, we believe crafts are all about conversation – the passing of skills and techniques from person to person down the ages. And we'd like our books to be part of that conversation.

To join in the conversation visit
↗ **www.how2crafts.com/contribute**

Talk to us at
↗ **www.twitter.com/how2crafts**

Welcome to a revival

Acrylic jewellery has been growing in popularity since the 1960's. Although it has, in the past, been associated with kitsch, throwaway designs, in more recent years there's been a growing number of jewellery designers who are interested in exploring the material's potential for more 'precious' pieces.

In this book, we start to explore methods of 'resist' dyeing acrylic. It can be difficult to achieve a good, deep colour on acrylic without using difficult to obtain 'carrier' chemicals, so I have recommended a particular Claret Red shade which I know works well.

If you enjoy making the acrylic jewellery in this book, you can carry on to experiment with other colours and shapes. Alternative methods of masking acrylic for resist dyeing include using Copydex, Art Masking Fluid , stickers and Masking tape. You can also polish the dye off certain areas, or use dip-dyeing.

A note on safety

Your dye should come with a safety data sheet that you should familiarise yourself with before making your jewellery.

Apart from this there are sensible precautions to be taken when handling dyes and chemicals, particularly in powder form:

- Avoid breathing in the powdered dye as it can produce an asthma type reaction. You may want to wear a dust mask.

- Wear surgical gloves and avoid prolonged skin contact, contact with the eyes or swallowing.

- Store your dye in clearly labelled containers out of reach of children, pets and away from food. You should treat dye powders and solutions with the same caution as domestic poisons, like strong cleaners, bleaches or medicines.

- It is recommended that if you are using utensils from the kitchen for dyeing that you subsequently keep them separate from utensils used for food preparation.

- Dispose of the dye solution responsibly.

Equipment

To make the jewellery described in this book you will need a flat work surface (a table or kitchen side will be fine) and a kitchen stove. You will also need the items listed below, and shown over the page. For details of where to obtain the more unusual items please see the list of suppliers on page 36.

Acrylic
- length of 8mm diameter clear cast round acrylic rod
- length of 15mm diameter half-round clear cast acrylic rod

Dye
- 25g of disperse dye: Dysperse Claret Red EBD
- bottle of white distilled vinegar
- bottle of washing-up liquid

Safety equipment
- safety spectacles
- rubber gloves
- apron

Jewellery supplies
- length of 1mm silver wire
- 1.2mm x 42cm silver omega necklet
- 10 x 4mm silver round two-hole beads
- length of 0.5mm Beadalon elasticity thread

Tools
- set square
- metal ruler
- small round-nosed pliers
- flat-nosed pliers
- half-round pliers
- wire cutters

- fine metal file
- wire cutters
- drill (pillar or hand drill and vice)
- vice (either attached to a work bench, or a portable vice as shown on page 8)
- 1mm drill bit
- 1.5mm drill bit
- 2.5mm drill bit
- bandsaw or coping saw with medium blade
- wet and dry paper, grades 120, 600 and 1200
- tube of Peek polishing compound (or a polishing motor, cotton polishing wheel and Vonax polishing compound)

Other equipment
- small elastic bands
- tube of Superglue

- tube of Araldite Rapide glue
- masking tape
- clip-on thermometer
- old toothbrush
- fine-point permanent marker pen
- piece of cardboard
- measuring jug (either plastic or glass will be fine)
- dessert spoon
- teaspoon
- small saucepan/small plastic bowl
- 2 litre saucepan
- small sieve (plastic or metal)
- large sieve (plastic or metal) to fit 2 litre saucepan (preferably with a handle)
- drying cloth (tea-towel/small towel)
- muslin cloth
- washing up sponge

1. The bracelet
Cutting and sanding

Note: *Many of the steps for making the bracelet, earrings and necklace are identical or very similar. For example, the pieces for all three need to be cut, sanded, polished, masked and dyed. If you are making all three items, you may want to do all the cutting, sanding, polishing, masking and dyeing at the same time.*

Measure 15mm from the end of the 15mm diameter half-round clear cast acrylic rod and mark a line with your permanent marker and set square (Fig 1). Secure the rod, wrapped in cardboard to protect it from getting scratched, in your vice and cut a 15mm square section off, following the line you have just drawn (Fig 2). As you're nearing the end of the cut, hold the piece to stop it breaking off before you've cut right

through the acrylic, in order to ensure a neat cut. Repeat until you have 10 beads.

Now begin sanding the cut ends of the beads with the coarsest grade wet and dry paper, dampened with a small amount of water. Holding the bead with the cut end facing down, being careful to keep the bead upright throughout, sand with a circular motion, pressing lightly (Fig 3). Continue with the coarse paper until you can no longer see any saw marks on the cut surface of the bead. This will probably take up to a minute. Next, move on to the medium grade, and then the fine grade (Fig 4). You'll only need a few strokes on both of these papers. When you're finished there'll be no visible score marks and the surface will be smooth to the touch and look slightly frosted.

Polishing and masking

Now to polish the cut pieces of acrylic. Put a blob of Peek polish on your piece of cardboard (Fig 5), and, holding the bead with the rough end facing the cardboard, polish the surface with a circular motion (Fig 6). Polishing should take no more than a couple of minutes. Check your progress every now and then by wiping the polishing compound off the bead and looking at the polished surface. When finished, you shouldn't be able to tell the difference between the polished surface and the rest of the acrylic (Fig 7).

Remove the excess polish with your cloth and wash the acrylic with washing up liquid to get all the polish off. Dry with your drying cloth.

Now wrap a small elastic band or two tightly around the centre of each bead, arranging them so there is an area of dense coverage in the centre of the bead, with more gaps at the edges (Fig 8). The aim is to create a tie-dye effect, with a clear strip in the middle of the bead, and more stripey bits either side. It's worth noting that even when you can't see any gaps between the strands by eye, the dye may still find a gap. (*Fig 8 shows the beads for the bracelet, earrings and necklace. As the dyeing process is identical for all the pieces it makes sense to dye them all together if you are making all three pieces of jewellery*).

Dyeing

When you buy disperse dye it should come with a safety data sheet. Familiarise yourself with this, and for your own safety, it is recommended that you wear rubber or surgical gloves, a full front-covering apron and safety spectacles. See also the safety precautions on page 4.

Measure two litres of water into your large saucepan. Add two teaspoons of distilled white vinegar and a squirt (roughly two teaspoons) of washing-up liquid. These help the dye to dissolve. Stir. Clip your thermometer on to the side of the saucepan, put the saucepan on the stove and heat to 45 degrees (Fig 9). Once you have reached this temperature, remove the saucepan from the heat.

Now sift one level dessert spoon of dye powder into your small saucepan (Fig 10). Be careful as the dye will stain – if you're worried about your work surfaces (particularly wooden ones) you should cover them with newspaper. Pour a small amount of the warm water you've just heated up onto the dye powder in your small saucepan (Fig 11). Stir well for about a minute, until the dye is fully dissolved. Now pour the dissolved dye back into the large saucepan of water (Fig 12), and again stir well until it is fully mixed in.

Place the prepared pieces of acrylic into your large sieve (Fig 13). Lower the sieve into the dye bath (Fig 14), and put the saucepan back on to the heat. While the pan is heating up, jiggle the sieve up and down to prevent the acrylic lying against the bottom of the sieve and leaving a 'sieve' pattern on the acrylic.

Heat up to approximately 90 degrees, making sure you don't exceed 95, (don't forget to jiggle the sieve continuously while heating), checking the temperature and depth of colour regularly. Remove the saucepan from the heat if it gets too hot. It should take about 15 minutes for a good depth of colour to be achieved.

When you are happy with the colour, remove the beads from the dye bath, and leave them till they cool to room temperature (Fig 15). It's important to keep moving the pieces, even as they cool, to prevent the pattern of the sieve being transferred on to the acrylic.

Now the exciting bit! Once the pieces have cooled to room temperature, you can remove the elastic bands and see what pattern you've created. Rinse well in running water to wash off the dye. Then wipe each piece with a washing-up sponge and detergent, rinse again and pat dry with a soft cloth. The dye can either be kept (once cooled) for use again, or if not, dispose of it responsibly.

You are now ready to finish your jewellery (Fig 16).

Drilling

When drilling acrylic, the two things to be careful of are overheating and the drill bit slipping and marking the surface (particularly when you're drilling on a sloping surface). To avoid overheating, always drill very slowly, a little at a time, withdrawing the drill bit fully each time, cleaning off the 'swarf' with an old toothbrush. To avoid the drill bit slipping on the surface of the acrylic (this only really matters when you are drilling on a sloping surface), start by drilling a small pilot hole, and make sure the drill bit is only sticking out of the end of the drill by 5mm or so to begin with. This reduces the amount by which the drill bit can bend, and therefore makes it less likely to slip.

Using your permanent marker pen, place a small dot in the centre top of each bead. Place the bead in your vice (Fig 17). Slowly drill all the way through the bead using a 1.5mm drill bit. If you are using a hand-held drill as we are here, and not a pillar drill, it might be worth getting a friend to check you are holding the drill completely vertical while drilling through the bead. Without an extra pair of eyes it's very hard to keep the hole parallel with the sides of the bead.

Finishing

Cut a metre or so of your Beadalon elasticity thread. Fold in half and put a small piece of masking tape over the folded end to stop it pulling through the beads. Thread both cut ends alternately through an acrylic bead and a silver bead (Fig 18) until you have 10 acrylic beads and 10 silver beads on your thread.

Pull the thread taut so there are no gaps between the beads, and tie a double knot (Fig 19), and then put a tiny dab of Superglue on the knot (Fig 20). You might need to enlist the help of a friend here, to pull the loose ends of the knot taut while you put a dab of Superglue on. Hold the knot taut while the glue dries, then cut the loose ends off. Pull the knot into a silver bead to hide it.

The finished bracelet. A strikingly modern and totally unique piece of jewellery.

2. The earrings
Sanding, polishing and dyeing

Note: As many of the steps for making the earrings, bracelet and necklace are identical or very similar, rather than repeating photographs, we refer you back to the process for the bracelet on pages 10–20, where we have shown the steps in full photographic detail.

Take your 8mm diameter clear acrylic rod, and cut two 3cm lengths with your bandsaw or coping saw. Now follow the steps for sanding, polishing and masking with rubber bands on pages 10–12. Dye the beads by following the instructions on pages 14–16. When cooled, remove the elastic bands and rinse the dye off.

Place one earring bead vertically in the vice, protecting it with cardboard as you did for the bracelet beads, and mark the centre top with your marker pen (Fig 21). Make a 1mm diameter drill hole approximately 5mm deep (Fig 22) – see page 18 for important information on drilling acrylic.

Next you need to make some ear-hooks. You can of course buy these ready-made, but in the spirit of craftsmanship (or craftswomanship!) I've included instructions for making them yourself.

Cut four 5cm lengths of 1mm silver wire with your wire cutters (Fig 23). File both ends with your fine file.

Make a little loop at one end with your small round-nosed pliers, about 2mm internal diameter (Fig 24).

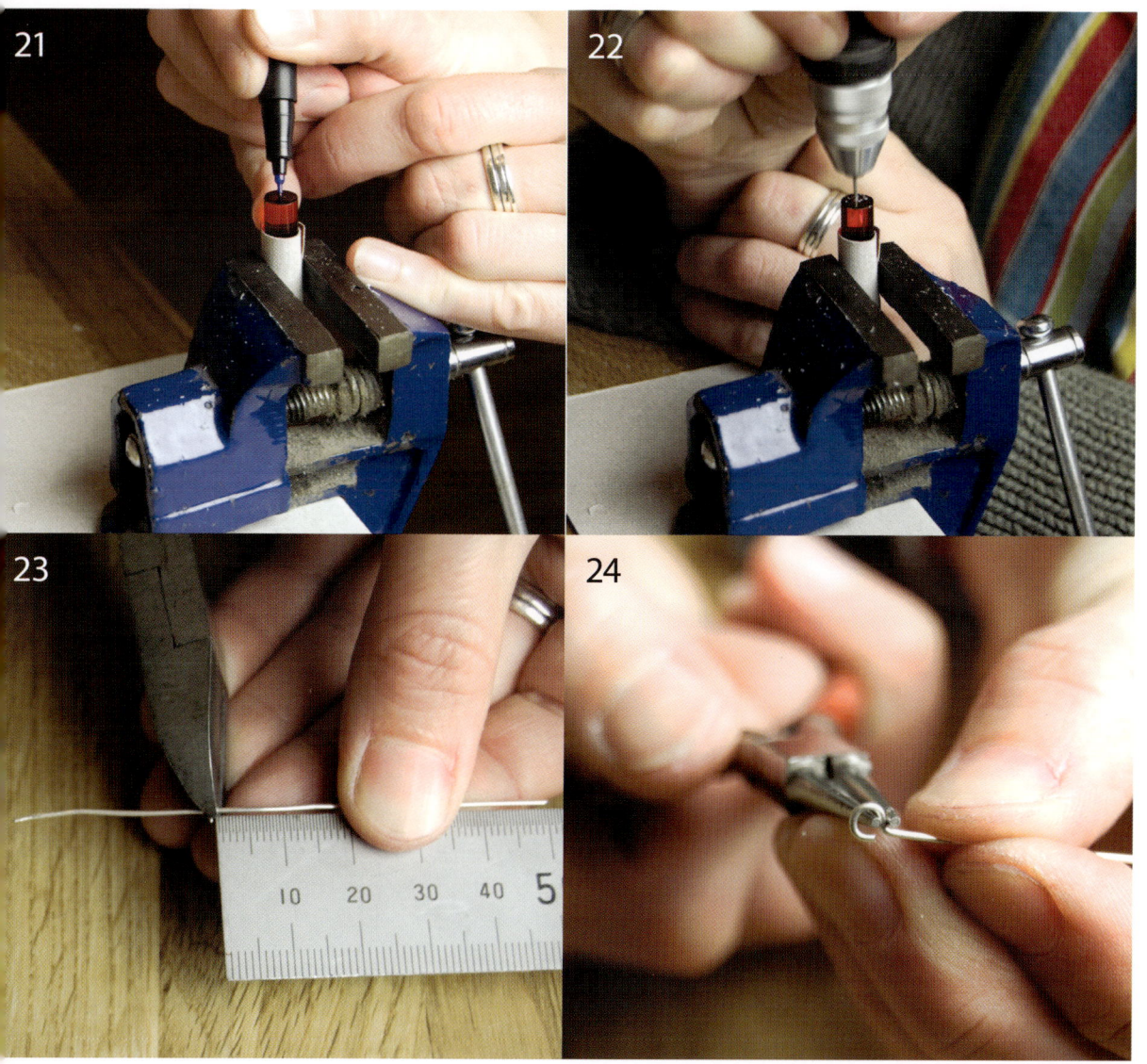

With a small piece of wet and dry paper, file the straight end of the wire, rounding it off (Fig 25), as this is the end that will go in your ear. Now with your half-round pliers, bend the wire below the small loop into a larger circle (Fig 26). This is best done in small steps rather than trying to make the circle with one big bend. Bend the end back slightly as shown in Figure 27. Repeat this process to create a second ear-hook.

Now you need to make the hooks that go in the end of the earrings and which attach on to your ear-hooks. Take one of the remaining 5cm pieces of 1mm silver wire and, using your round-nosed pliers, make a 2mm internal diameter loop at one end as you did for the ear-hooks (see Fig 24 on the previous page). Cut the wire 5mm away from the loop. Repeat this process to create a second little hook.

Mix up a small amount of Araldite, put a tiny blob on the cut end of the 5mm loop you have just made, and holding the circle end in your flat nosed pliers, glue the hook into the hole at the end of your earrings (Fig 28). Leave the glue to dry.

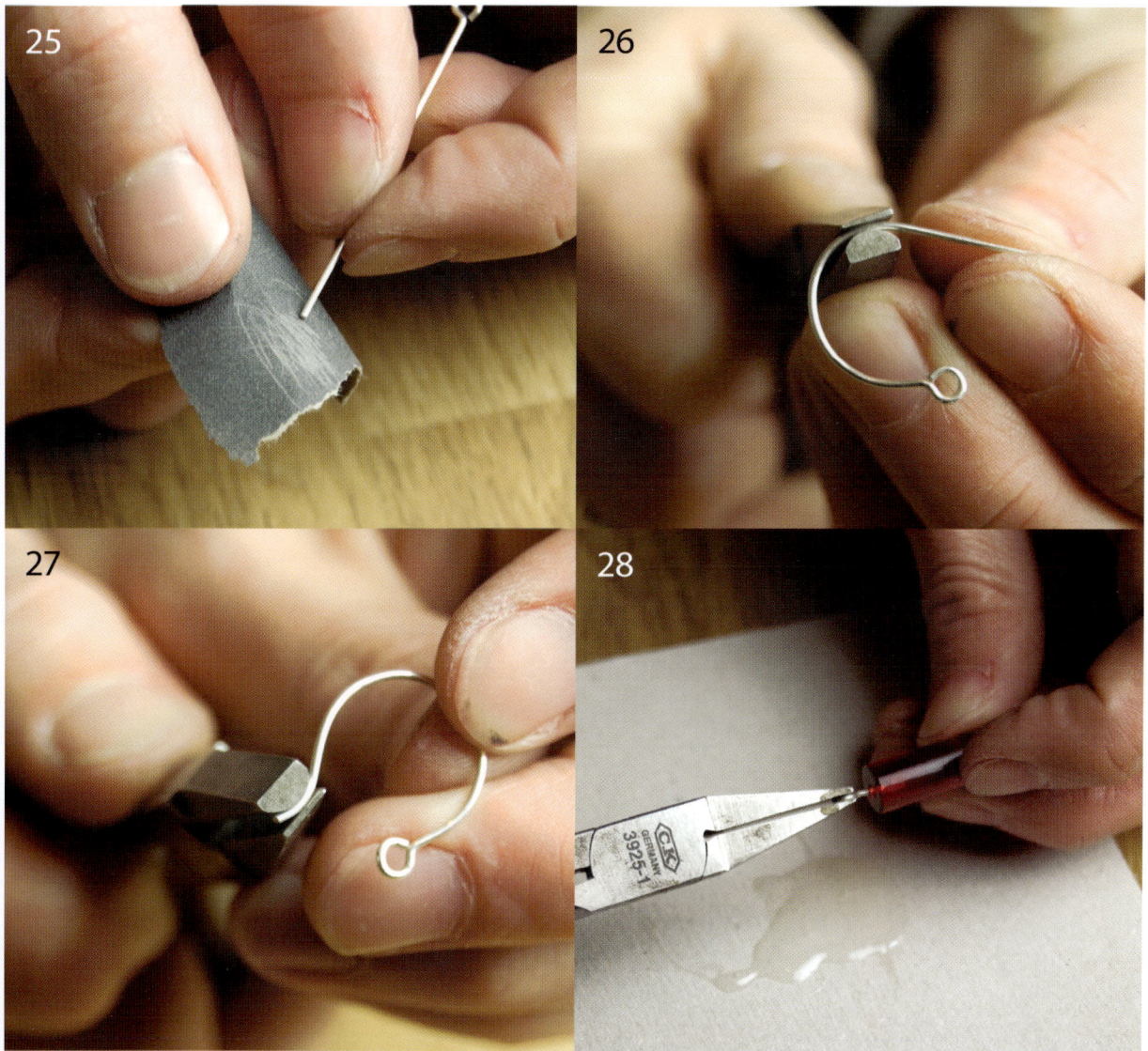

Using your flat-nosed pliers, open the loop on the ear hook and attach the earring. Close up the loop on the ear hook.

Your earrings are now finished!

3. The necklace
Sanding, polishing and dyeing

Note: *As many of the steps for making the necklace, earrings and bracelet are identical or very similar, rather than repeating photographs, we refer you back to the process for the bracelet on pages 10–20, where we have shown the steps in full photographic detail.*

Take the 15mm diameter half round rod, and cut a 3cm length pendant with your coping saw. Follow the steps for sanding, polishing and masking with rubber bands on pages 10–12.

Dye the pendant, following the instructions on pages 14–16. Cool and rinse your pendant.

Now you need to drill a hole to thread your pendant onto the necklet (see page 18 for important information on drilling acrylic). Mark a point on the side of the curved side of the pendant, 1cm down from the top (Fig 29). Hold the pendant horizontally in your vice, protected by cardboard. Place a 1.5mm drill bit in your drill, with only 5mm or so showing. Carefully drill a short pilot hole (Fig 30). Then reset the drill bit so about 20mm is showing and drill all the way through with the 1.5mm drill bit. Now following the pilot hole you have just drilled, drill a 2.5mm hole right through to the other side (Fig 31).

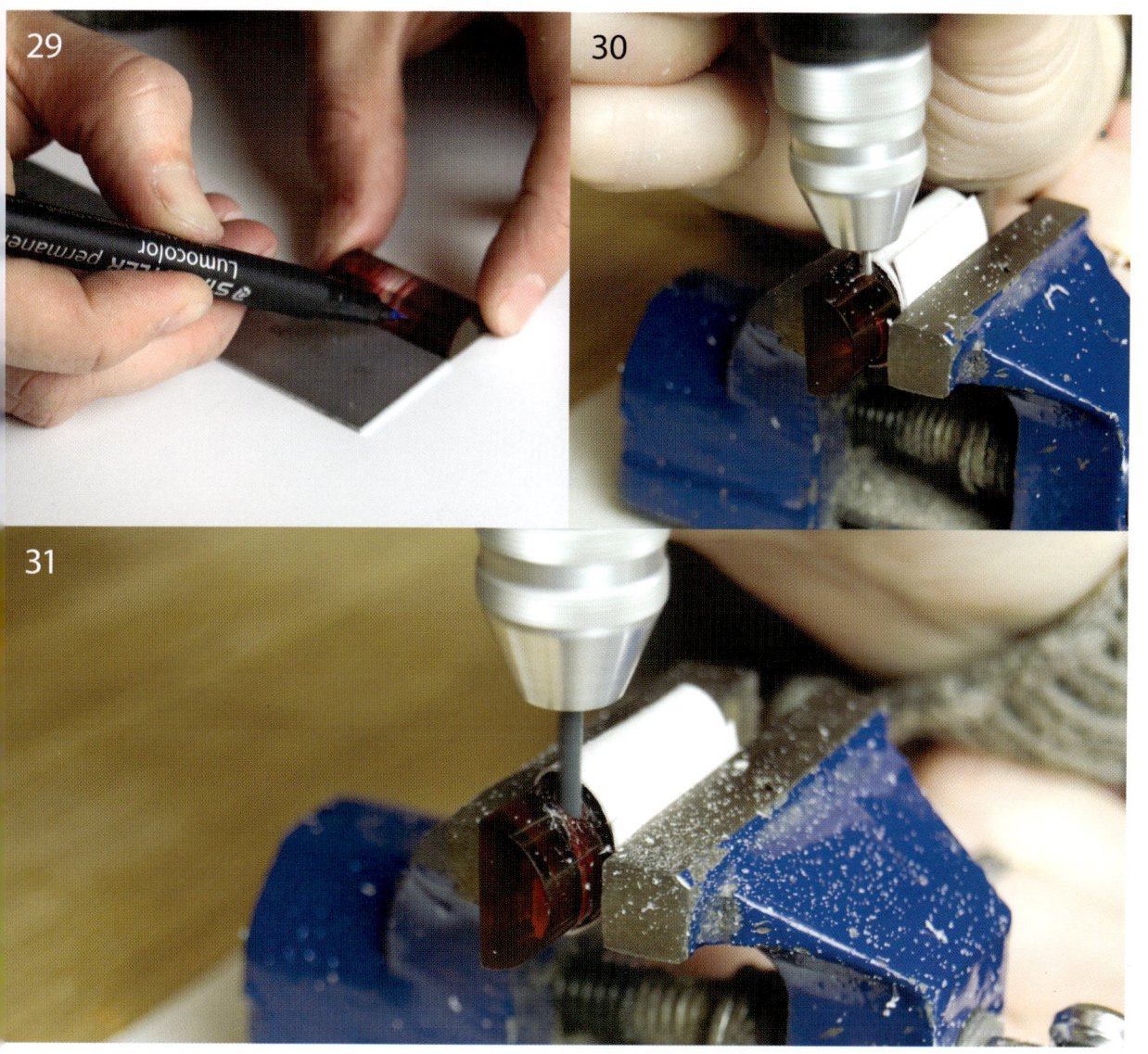

Thread your pendant onto your silver omega necklet. The set is now complete!

Taking your ideas further

Hopefully this book will have given you a good grounding in the basics of making and dyeing acrylic jewellery. Acrylic is available in many different shapes and sizes (see the suppliers list at the end of this book for details of where to purchase it), and the designs you can make are only limited by your imagination. We'd love to see what you make – and if you send us a photo of your design you'll be in with a chance of getting yourself into print in this very book!

To upload photos and comments, go to
↗ **www. how2crafts.com/contribute**

Happy making!

Suppliers

I have listed some UK suppliers on the right. For suppliers in your area, google the item or material you are looking for and your nearest town or city. Try these search terms:

- Jewellery supplies
- "clear cast acrylic rod"
- dysperse or disperse dyes
- hardware supplies

If you would like to recommend suppliers in your area please do let us know via our website at ↗ **www.how2crafts.com**. We will then list them in future editions of this book.

UK suppliers

Dyes
I bought my dye – 25 grams of dysperse claret red EBD 25g from Kemtex Educational Supplies
↗ **www.kemtex.co.uk**

Silver, beads and elastic thread
Cookson Precious Metals
↗ **www.cooksongold.com**

Acrylic
↗ **www.ensinger.ltd.uk**

Tools and hardware
Available from any good hardware shop.

Other books by how2crafts

Make your own Soap

Joy James.
An exceptionally easy to follow, step-by-step photographic instruction book on making soap.
A best-seller.

Felt Biscuits

Ouissi Gresty.
This book takes you through how to make these amazing felt sculptures – the next big thing for those bored of crocheted cupcakes...

Simple Printmaking

Sarah Roberts.
Print your own gorgeous cards, gift tags and wrapping paper. By award-winning printmaker Sarah Roberts.

How to make a Felt Handbag

Lisa Slinn.
This delightful little book is so well written and illustrated that it makes the seemingly difficult process of felting extremely simple.

Make your own Handbag, Clutch Bag and Purse

Emma Castle.
See a bag you love? Don't buy it, make it! Full step-by-step instructions.

All books available from
↗ **www.how2crafts.com**

About the author

Sarah Packington was born in London, and studied Wood, Metal, Ceramics and Plastics at Brighton Polytechnic.

She has been designing and making acrylic and silver jewellery since 1993, and her work can be seen at MIMA in Middlesborough, Leeds City Art Gallery, and Aberdeen Art Gallery amongst other shops and galleries around Britain.

She loves to experiment with different ways to get colour and pattern into her jewellery.